Snow day

rob mclennan

SPUYTEN DUYVIL
New York City

ISBN 978-1-963908-58-9

My single motivation is authentic experience. I can only approach it by telling stories.

Richard Froude, *Your Love Alone Is Not Enough*

Fragment plus fragment equals fragmentation and we can work harder with what we have left of what we have lost or what we have left of what we never had.

Lesle Lewis, *Rainy Days on the Farm*

snow day

Here is a system. Time pours from its mouth.
Lisa Robertson, *The Weather*

How do most people live without any thought? There are
many people in the world,—you must have noticed them
in the street,—how do they live? How do they get strength
to put on their clothes in the morning?
Emily Dickinson

The owl puts none of this into language
Roo Borson & Kim Maltman,
The Transparence Of November / Snow

First thing this morning, Christine and I each receive an email regarding the cancellation of buses across the school board. The warmer temperatures bring freezing rain. We live too close to the school for the cancellations to affect us. I still bundle both children for Rose's drop-off, for her to begin another full day of junior kindergarten. Neither cancelled, nor snow: what kind of snow day is that?

Anna Gurton-Wachter responds to my email. Monty Reid responds to my email. Nikki Sheppy responds to my email. Stephen Brockwell responds to my email. Neil Flowers responds to my email. Pearl Pirie responds to my email. David O'Meara responds to my email. Annick MacAskill responds to my email. Christine McNair responds to my email. Sarah Burgoyne responds to my email. Shazia Hafiz Ramji responds to my email. Christine McNair responds to my email. natalie hanna responds to my email. Christine McNair responds to my email. Christine McNair responds to my email. Christine McNair responds to my email. Christine McNair responds to my email.

Ian Williams responds to a photograph of my home office: "Don't you feel perpetually overwhelmed?"

"I saw the photo of your writing desk and wanted to close the door."

When I repeat a story, it is because I am close to learning something new about it.

The willingness to explore an already familiar terrain. Freezing rain.

For Rose, it barely registers. Our toddler, Aoife, unimpressed. A grimace.

My father's boyhood story of his hyperactive dog who lost a leg to machinery. My father's boyhood story of his hyperactive three-legged dog.

The snow and the driveway and the entire fabric of nature. Out of memory, out of sight. I will not leave the house.

When I repeat a story. A blind spot. Listen.

Reading Kate Greenstreet, I'm held by the integrity of her collage and coherence. "All our bones, and the mountains." Rereading Rosmarie Waldrop, the linear abstracts of her *Blindsight*. I am attempting, yet again, to describe.

Snowmen, sizzle. A break in the tide. Are we meant to apologize.

For the weather, I mean. The snow. A Canadian stereotype. I'm sorry.

Minus twenty-two, prior to wind-chill. How low.

As Nelson Ball wrote, bird tracks on hard snow. At this level of cold, the only evidence.

The backyard trestled by paw-tracks. Akin to Billy, wandering the neighbourhoods of Bill Keane's *The Family Circus*. Birds, flurry. A rabbit. The occasional skunk.

Last summer, another parent in the playground offered: there is more than one rabbit.

American poet Claire Schwartz tweets a screen-shot of one of her poems, featured in the latest issue of *Bennington Review*. "What is a nation which does not save / poetry? What is a poem but the gathering / of lines?"

A layering of dust. Sparkles. A body can be.

A year earlier, I wove Emily Dickinson's hair into a poem. In the Archives and Special Collections at Amherst College, a lock of her chestnut brown set under glass. Her only known photograph.

Mount Holyoke College, formerly Mount Holyoke Female Seminary. In South Hadley, Massachusetts, where Emily Dickinson shared classroom space with the Robertson sisters, who were far from their family home in Sherbrooke, Quebec. Margaret Murray, who would later become a successful novelist, and Mary, called home by their father, for the sake of marriage. Mary, who married, resettled in Glengarry County and produced four healthy children. One of her sons, the Rev. Charles Gordon, published novels under the pseudonym Ralph Connor, and became one of the most successful Canadian writers of the period. A novelist from Glengarry, who would also become father and grandfather to novelists.

That I could write. That I could also write. As I am writing.

Sacred Emily. From Gertrude Stein's 1913 notebook: "Foolish is foolish is."

The first impulse with fresh snow: to make a mark upon it.

In an email, Samuel Ace responds: "Emily haunts the whole valley on that side of the river—from Amherst to South Hadley. There's a specific New England interiority—brought on by the snow and the quiet of the woods—that I feel so strongly when I'm there. One has to scratch one's way into being."

I sit at my desk. I sit in the living room, surrounded by toys. The snowplows scrape new furrows across a half-century of traffic. I sit on the downstairs couch, surrounded by toys. I sit at the kitchen island, which, attached to the wall, is more specifically a peninsula. Surrounded by toys. Underneath the highchair, green toddler socks, abandoned. Monster stickers, princess stickers, flower stickers, held to the living room hardwood. There are rooms between us. The children scatter and thread.

To scratch one's way.

Shovel, shovel, gasp. Bag of salt distributed along cement steps, the walkway, drive. Snowplow carves the length. How Canadian is our winter, really. How, really.

"Emily Dickinson was, in her lifetime," @KishWidyaratna tweets, "perhaps more widely known as a gardener than poet."

Via the Harvard Library website, I flip through Dickinson's *Herbarium*, circa 1839-1846. A sequence of greenery that retains its colour.

The foundation people are here. Mr. Foundation. A man named Keith that Christine would not allow me to call "Keith Foundation." Is there a Mrs. Foundation? A Ms.? They jackhammer through layers of frozen soil.

The late captain's 19th century house in Cobourg, Ontario, adapted into current bed and breakfast, where we once stayed in the "Mrs. Fortune" room. As I said at the time: "Mrs. Fortune: the mother of many Miss Fortunes." Ahem.

Stephen Brockwell responds to an email. We discuss the possibility of childcare. This happens, also.

According to Google, people also ask:

> How do you get a snow day?
> Is it a snow day?
> How much snow does it take for a school to close?
> Are the buses cancelled?

When I was young, my mother and I huddled over kitchen radio. Sometimes the school board would cancel the buses, and occasionally my bus might skip our concession, if the turn from Fraser Road wasn't safe, wasn't worth it. The lone stop on our road.

Accumulating rain, our front-yard snowman is revealed. A poorly-shaped mound of snow accrued a month's worth of flurries, now subject to freezing drizzle.

An official *Ottawa Citizen* certificate somewhere in my archives to prove I survived Ottawa's record snowfall of January 1971. Forty-seven years ago. I wasn't a full year old. While these certificates were free to newspaper subscribers, my maternal grandfather, who worked as a printer for the paper, collected individual certificates for everyone in the family.

I have one, my uncle had one, my mother had one, etcetera.

In December, Rose remained a day home from school. A sick day. She and her younger sister, slowly, inevitably, dismantled the house. Over Christmas, the same. Too cold to leave. A cabin fever that sets. As slow as lead type.

Via twitter, the Emily Dickinson Museum posts a short video of the snow falling in and around her garden. Such silence. Hashtag: New England winter.

Who reads poems in the age of Twitter? Who reads books?

As the children, with blankets and bedsheets, assemble a cave. The days we chose not to venture forth.

Twitter is so over, dude. Go back to 2013. What are we even doing?

By then, I'd long misplaced my MySpace password.

Minus twenty, minus twenty-one. Minus twenty-two.

If I were to scratch these lines on an envelope.

At times, we live dangerously close to falling.

Everything dies. I want to hold hands with the millennia.

Muriel Spark wrote: "We all have a fatal flaw."

The jackhammer vs. the toddler's nap. As necessity requires, her sister's bed. The difference of one room, further from the noise.

Ladies and gentlemen: place your bets.

My slow and silent retreat.

Right on schedule, our handyman returns. Unfinished corners of the basement, bare blocks of cinder concrete. To insulate against the cold.

Holes chewed through sunroom ceiling. That fucking squirrel.

Brooklyn poet Anna Vitale asks, rhetorically, in *Detroit Detroit* (2017): "To build / Or not build [.]"

Make your final bets, please.

Someday we will tell the story. In all manner of speech.

There are certain books that, reread every decade, revitalize. The words shape to your situation, your experience. Reflect.

Daniel Lanois' *Acadie* (1989). An album that hasn't aged, although I have.

Some might say, "There is a poem in here, somewhere." This, already.

I can't remember spring. Inspirational gifs, and email delays.

This is not what I asked for. Less complex than it seems.

The sidewalks plowed. In time for the rain.

Count the remaining weeks: forty-eight years old. Party 'till I break a hip.

Where we live on the continent. To remain or return to familiar terrain.

What my archive, accumulates. I pack boxes and folders for couriers to collect, sent forth into Calgary. All the way to the foothills.

Correspondence, notebooks, notebooks, postcards. Manuscripts. All apology.

Cole Swensen, *On Walking On* (2017): "If you walk in complete silence, other beings are not forced // to rearrange themselves into unrecognizable things."

Ottawa Valley cold. Ontario cold. Cold anywhere. An approaching Arctic air mass.

What one might wish to unfold.

There are a variety of Emily Dickinson accounts on Twitter, including StonedEmilyDickinson (@1830-1886) with the Twitter bio "Poetry.

White Dresses. Alone Time. Baking Bread." and E. Dickinson's Dress (@280MainStreet) with the bio "cotton fabric with mother-of-pearl buttons, partly machine made, partly hand-stitched."

I mention these not as judgement, but out of curiosity. The truth is out there.

What fragments, this. The #CanLit dumpster fires rage. Another day, another notification that turns the community against itself. Disenchantments abound. How are you not seeing this?

Please note, for your records:

a) Racism is bad.
b) Violence in any form is bad.
c) This includes sexual violence.
d) If someone says they have been the target of any or all of these, that person should be believed.
e) Fairness, by very definition, must apply equally to both sides.

Was that so difficult?

Now flights may be cancelled due to the rain. Where would I go?

Boils over. What can't be said. After two weeks-plus of minus twenty degrees Celsius, the walk becomes bearable. The onset of rain.

Hamstead Heath. The view over London protected by law. The Billings Estate, which includes a panorama of Parliament. Emily Dickinson's garden.

From our front window, draft. The cat's frantic chatter; sparrows our front yard maple, the crabapple. Our mailman's swift tread.

All our bones, and the asphalt. The neighbourhood glistens.

All the snow we could gather.

When I saw my school bus not make the turn, I knew our road was too icy. I knew it meant I could remain home.

No page but the page. Remains blank.

The snow coats our yard. Wake up. Alta Vista otherwise traffic-thick. The roads today, terrible.

The snow coats the car. Three inches. Extra-thick gloves. Christine turns the ignition, settles; blasts the heat, defrost. Scrapes windshield. We address each other in signals.

A twitter account for Emily Dickinson lyrics. A twitter account for out of context Anne Carson lines, specifically from her *Autobiography of Red* (1998). The poems, as Jack Spicer wrote, can no better live on their own than can we.

How much is too much? The Snow Report features daily online reports on snowfall across Canada, set specifically for those who ski. Resort stats, base depths, number of lifts, acreage and open runs.

It speaks not to driving conditions, or possible accidents. It speaks not to bus or school cancellations or road closures. It speaks not to what lies beneath. It speaks not to the silence.

Air duct cleaning services. Ten years of unsolicited phone calls. The no-contact list, please.

Bring your secrets to light. May they burn.

On this day in 1773. In 1304. In 1955. Words. Feel lost under flurries.

Lightweight. Whiplash wind and snowy curls.

Retweet Kaveh Akbar. Retweet Erin Wunker. Retweet Eaton Hamilton. Retweet Eve L. Ewing. Retweet Natalee Caple. Retweet Hazel Millar. Retweet Natalie Eilbert. Retweet Metatron Press. Retweet Zoe Whittall. Retweet Amal El-Mohtar. Retweet Astro Poets. Retweet Christine McNair, the rare time she does tweet. We want significance, relevance. We wish to engage. We want an end to hostilities. We want an end to the dark ends of silence. To remember why we love, why we love poems, why we love writing. To return to that joy of creation, community. Connection.

I want to feel the love I want to love the poems I want the poems that sing and breathe and rage I want the giving not the taking.

Return to small. Attempt, once more, to discover. What we came here to do. Revisit the idea. Revitalize. Sketch out. Absorb. Why we write in the first place.

Polyvocality is not cacophony. Is not a threat. A thread. Why can't we listen.

To no longer feel exhausted.

Sometimes doing nothing and doing something exist concurrently, in a single gesture.

As Rev. Charles Gordon wrote of his mother's youth in his *Postscript to Adventure: The Autobiography of Ralph Connor* (1938): "A few months later a deputation from the Board of Directors came to Sherbrooke to invite Mary Robertson to become the principal of Mount Holyoke. She was then about twenty-two years old. She was eager to go, but not quite sure of herself. Her father, who had noticed the frequent visits of a young Highland missionary working among the Scottish emigrants settled at Lingwick in the Lake Megantic district, advised against her going."

Walk Rose to school, flurried. The crossing guard raises her sign and sets forth.

My maternal great-grandfather who, once retired, did the same back in Kemptville. Rain, snow or shine. Those that still recall "Papa Swain" at the ready, protector of school-children.

In whose footprints we step. An infinite line.

By the front step. Unfamiliar animal tracks.

When we talk of the weather. There, on the tip of my tongue. The kid from *A Christmas Story*.

Tongue-lashed. A kettle of boiling water. Help me.

Scrape, pathway, walk. Salt.

Out into the snow. Children, staccato. When we talk of the weather.

Sidewalk, sidewalk, steps.

Such solitude. I seek what is not yet visible.

The ends of the drive.

I am unable to write in complete silence. For six months, a single cd on repeat. Does it matter which one? Press play. Press play. Press play.

Ignore the video floating around social media: "Deals with the Devil: A Brief Musical History." This, too, shall pass.

The city plants saplings I've seen municipal snowplows decapitate. The city giveth, and taketh away. The right hand has no idea what the left hand is doing.

The air outside.

Of Canadians, they say: the snow. A language we use. In winter, where the nights are long.

I was back on the farm. My morning school bus, orange at the end of the road.

I was back in the schoolyard, toddler in tow. The rain had long stopped, and what snow remained was perfect for molding. The snow-forts were melting. "Not forts," Rose claimed, but "clubs."

If this is but an afterthought.

I would rather remain indoors. This has not changed.

Today in history.

When I repeat a story. Clickbait.

The winter days my mother had to force us out. "I don't want to see you until ___." A pain upon cheeks as we tore through the snow. Such cold. Wood smoke from the furnace up the chimney rolling out and down to the ground to swirl tumbleweed slow across yard and disperse.

"If you saw a bullet hit a bird—and he told you he wasn't shot—you might weep at his courtesy..."—Emily Dickinson

Mary Robertson Gordon (c. 1822—1890). Sister to a novelist, a Member of Parliament and two lawyers. Further in his autobiography, Rev. Charles Gordon wrote: "She was a saint, but a gay and gallant saint. She had no fear of the forest. On her pony, a baby perched before her on the pommel of her saddle and another on the way, she would gallop along the trails winding through the forest, skirting bogholes, jumping logs—once she made her pony leap over a slumbering cow—with the bark of a fox or the long howl of a wolf sounding in her ears."

Known for her poise, intelligence, fearlessness. Remembered for her kindness.

A neighbour, two doors down, warns of a backyard coyote sighting. Alta Vista and Palen. They care nothing for our children, Christine reminds, but don't let the cat out.

The year the fishers came, and my mother's cat disappeared. Coyotes are good, I've been told, for keeping down the mice population. The snow and the wilderness encroach upon our encroachments. How to coexist, exactly. I don't know.

Via Facebook, another parent offers: there is more than one coyote.

I don't remember who wrote: 'it is better to hold your funeral before you die.' A quote that sticks to my memory like butter. Unattributed.

Unattributed, also: "When you should be asleep, but twitter."

January 2, 1999, when a snowstorm dropped thirty-nine centimetres of snow on Toronto. A series of storms kept rolling in. Within two weeks, a state of emergency, as Mayor Mel Lastman called in the army. Dig, baby, dig.

January, 1998, when an ice storm caused major damage across Eastern Ontario and southern Quebec, revealing the poor quality of Quebec's electrical grid.

March 4, 1971, when forty-seven centimetres of snow fell on Montreal, made worse by winds up to 110 km/hour. The drifts kept rolling, rolling in.

What else do you wish to know.

Such fierce winds through Pyeongchang County, South Korea. Enough to knock Olympic hopefuls from their path, pushed twenty feet into the air. Their snowboards become sails.

The mid-season opener of CW's *DC Legends of Tomorrow* that shows their resident historian, Dr. Nathaniel "Nate" Heywood, reach for his quick-at-hand copy of Ralph Connor's 1901 novel, *The Man from Glengarry*, in an attempt to discover hints to the location of his time-displaced teammates.

Why would he seek them in fiction?

We begin to doubt your credentials as a historian, Commander Steel.

Christine responds to an email. We discuss the possibilities of childcare. This too, happens.

Dead at ninety-five. Dead at sixty-three. Dead at forty. Dead at seventy-five. Dead at thirty-two. Dead at sixty. Dead at eighty-seven. Dead at seventy. Scroll through the obituaries, seeking out names, and particulars. Scroll through the connections. What am I seeking. The names of the dead and their angular pinpoints: birth, marriage, children. Remnants.

When a miracle is not a miracle. How close to your grammar.

Despite the weather, Canada Post delivers a handwritten note from Brooklyn poet and filmmaker Stephanie Gray. At times, one forgets such things existed: a note sketched by hand, and offered through snail mail.

The note's verso: Brooklyn "Mapnote," pinpointing Flatbush, Midwood, Bushwick, Borough Park.

Pattie McCarthy, *margerykempething* (2017): "this sentence is from several failed attempts [.]"

Ralph Connor, the Rev. Charles Gordon. What they called "Indian Lands," Glengarry County. Nearly a century later and two miles west: this is where I come in.

Stones in her pockets. Off-screen, I place eggs in the Instant Pot, set a dozen for hard-boil. Off-screen, the children sit quietly, flip through their books.

Michael Harris' poem "Death and Miss Emily," from *Grace* (1978). On The Porcupine's Quill, Inc. blog in November, 2017, intern Stephanie Small mentions the poem, and writes of "The act of going back, of probing a topic like a sore tooth […]." Of which she was very much in favour.

Snow. What I know of it, falls.

The storm not a metaphor but situated in fact. Shovels the weight of the walk.

The penitent, kneels. Anna Gurton-Wachter: "The mouth is a whisper of an earlier event."

Within days, temperatures rise. The rain. From minus twenty-three to plus-eight in the space of a week. The snow evaporates with such force it steams, producing fog from the asphalt. It lifts.

Somewhere in-between / cloud

I like my poems to look me in the eye.
Ben Purkert, *For The Love Of Endings*

She had read nearly everything. Or imagined it
Marthe Reed

for/after Marthe Reed,
dearly missed,

I could not think clearly, so I began to write.

I was trying to write an elegy. Contrails. What is our relationship to the human body? A land we stand upon and spoil. Tales of villainy, richness. Darkness. The earth provides.

Colonizers
name

and rename.

No longer of being,
but belonging.

How, then,
to write?

Truth lies
in the destruction.

Forest for the trees.

"Nomad," she once wrote, "belonging accidentally."

That which surrounds.
Through the razor-sharp.
The speed of cloth.
The length of a sentence.

A placeholder title. *I was trying to write an elegy.*

The path resists. How many times can you fail the speaker.

Still alive in Ottawa,
still alive in Poughkeepsie,
still alive in Great Barrington.

We drove out once to see her. Rolled up their incline: the campus, the cemetery across. So many questions, covered in cow hide. An ending is so rarely final.

Mary Oliver directed: Be astonished.

John Newlove: let the measure fall / where it may.

This is not the green grass. This is not horizon.

Peter Van Toorn: where you can smell the poem in a thing for miles.

Marthe Reed: how many times / more excruciating // the charm of / revelation [.]

Say your piece, in the free form boxes.
Click to send.

Not enough to complain.
Not enough to poem.

I was trying to write an elegy.

Amid the shorn. Amid the "drastically collective." Amid the forest
for the trees. Amid the limitations of language codified. Amid the
self-denial. Amid the sheltering of difference. Amid the multitude of
beings, "clamoring for our scientific, political, and artistic attention."
Amid my burnt feet, paused before the same grass. Amid the guilt of
poetry and the pleasures of the text. Amid the many countries, distant
or near. Amid the memories of which for whom we still.

This is neither landscape nor portrait.

I don't know. Begin. I am I as we are *something something*. In this.

I am trying to write an elegy. She spoke volumes.

The introduction of property, and the unforgiving line.

Tears down
colloquialisms, as rough
shod as these leaves.

A collective
contrition.

Echolocate:
thoughts and prayers.

For every action:

Equal,
and opposite.

To write a line around an absence. Shape it. Ruins, ruined. Causal. Perpetual slight-of-hand. Nature, as she writes. Industrial. Outside, separate. Would they just join hands. A convulsion of class, and crisis. This is all connected. Sing with me.

A love of inch-ness.
How would you know
the world ends. How would you love.
The body,
like the letter, rarely separate.

The disconnect, bleeds.
One upon another.
A mutilation that reads,
articulates. Rankles. Does this spark
joy? Speak, in a transparent fragment.

Pastoral
a modernist

design: the
disconnect

between human
and nature,

that diminishes
both,

and understands
neither.

The universe is expanding. Recycling bins. My lungs are full.

This god
-awful place.

The land
bears witness.

Frames, and conditions. A glossary of sabotage. One buries the lead.

A loose canon.

Regulating
the field.

A small
comportment.

I was trying to write an elegy. A kind of numbness. Neither condition nor flaw. Water, through these handmade books. I cry out, walking. If one could summarize a beginning.

As Plato says: we write things down in order to forget.

Distraction: we
knew this.

Disarticulate
trees.

"[N]ot as distance," she wrote, "but as intimacy."

Covid lines

I Have Nothing to Say But I can say it very well.
Nihilist Spasm Band, "WHAT ABOUT ME" (1992)

for my fifty-first year,

i don't know what poetry is
or why i'm loyal to it
(if) i want clarity
if i can pursue a different
honesty that way

the thoughts i have
     Marion Bell, *austerity*

     I like that death is plural. Keeps happening.
          Anna Gurton-Wachter, *Utopia Pipe Dream Memory*

*

When I turned forty, Phil Hall offered: turning forty
is first looking back. What, then, at fifty?

Am I waiting for the ground to shake?

*

Based on actual events. A science
that sticks in the throat. Fifty years

to the day.

*

A pantheon of passcodes, gods. A pinch
of salt or a trick with a knife. There

so the colour won't run.

*

I call my mother: mum. I call her silence,
dead these past ten years. A stray fact,

impossible to remove.

*

The cold, from my bones. I am seeking the cold.

*

Half a century in, I have shirts older
than youthful contemporaries.

To refine the waves. A guarantee
of creative indecision.

To paraphrase Don McKay: fuck your provocations;

get me a beer.

*

What the hell are you on about.

*

Mary Ann Samyn reminds us
that it was Gaston Bachelard who reminded us

that it is we who are the curators

of our own images. The way
my heart stops,

like a country.

*

A counterclaim
of birds.

*

This policy is, by no means. Half a lifetime
since my twenty-fifth birthday,

singing loudly in a pub. Three sheets
to the wind. The conceptual language

of presence.

*

I put my foot down. A sentence
is enough.

*

The overlay

of language on land. The question
of which came first,

and the imprecisions each leave
across the other.

*

The great silence

of the poetic line.

*

In a year that left us

speechless.

blindness : poems for the left hand,

for Zane Koss,

I am learning that there are things we can only talk about

underwater that there is a struggle in only being able to see

> one of your lifetimes
> at a time
>
> of always sitting in the same
> seat in the theater

while the congress of you watches.
> Tanya Holtland, *Requisite*

1.

A formulation of the language.

This gentle fog. My right eye, cataracts.
Surgical delay: pandemic,

lacuna. A hardtack
annum.

2.

Can see you, there. Resurface,
steel rail. Trace walls with fingertips.

Neither water
nor edge.

Late father's slippers keep
my toes intact. Two breaks

are enough.

3.

The self, is. If you want a picture. Here
is what I believe.

As far as the eye. This
diversity of forms. The absence

is what stands.

covid lines

You know, sunsets are violently beautiful.
Etel Adnan, *Shifting the Silence* (2020)

the season is the air
near water full of crows
Pattie McCarthy

*

To consider a clear idea of a word,
you should listen to that word.

*

The issue hardly one of speech,
nor might it be solution.

*

This pandemic, chaos. A unity
of shameless hours.

What they write in the snow

My earliest memory of my daughters they
will have forgotten, which is not the same
as not having known.

> Kate Bolton Bonnici, *Night Burial* (2020)

Before the alphabet, there was the house.

> Claire Schwartz, "Lecture on the History of the House"

a scrapture, thus—

        unzipped coat, no hat; and mismatched gloves,
a lecture out the door; across
                    , a passage
   stripped; the second clause

of an otherwise sentence:

*

of powder, slush   ; canonical thinking

   : other words for snow,

: a bluster, white-out
, antithetical plume , a swish

        of children, house; the day

is spilling,

blatant heat,   a warmth
    of dissolute,

*

on the way out the door I was a bridge; I was
an ogre
        , shovel: squared

           the sweet
           subconscious

neighbour pulls a car out; waves,

    I carve a path,

*

this alphabet speaks   to the passing,
        parade
           of utter functions,

hardbound, wind: aberration, abrasion,
     shapes the backyard; what lay

                                        below,

to hold a face, or gesture;   rains,

                 beguile, baffle; blankets, this:

a treacle, lantern,   south-paw; broken wheelbarrow,
new pair of gloves,

*

such cold, metallic surface; new snow,

the closed system
                 of suburban landscape,

simulcast,   perpetual; bodies in motion
                remain,

, one lifts her hands

*

in this pandemic year: an utter absence
of snow days,
                labyrinthine—lockdowns pause,

and pause,

e-tethered; math scores, reading   , geographic site
irrelevant; half-expect

four   hundred kilometres

                , of hunger, enlightenment;

an absence of wholeness,

                      snowfall, settles

      unthinkable angles,

  *

I write to you from, from this—   , a quick thaw
       , temperate destruction

boots on the ground; boots on the ground with ice,
with spikes,

            for clear protection,

sand, or salted surface,

  *

peaks   of unresolved contradiction,
the shape of transition,

              translated: each phrase
      across the hedgerows;

the clothesline; linearity
      our black squirrels scuttle,   dart:

snow   as social function;   what is art,

the very principle of change,

    , icy footfalls, pattern; sidewalk where
Christine concussed, some

two years prior,

our driveway   held
    beyond capacity,

*

Jordan Davis tweets: two things can be true

who said   that true poetry is the prayer
of lyric, confession

                            , woodland; float,

amid the climates of the accident, and
the document,

hold: as responsive a state as any,

*

melts,   the small packs, blue   now
                      , into evening, snow

shall bring such peace,

if I am less   the only numerous,

picture the clearing;

picture the method of weather,

a weather of grey-white; a weather of shale,

two black birds ride the gate

a view of the uncommon

an uncorrected proof of birds

abandoned mittens, scarf

the moon struck down in flakes, in icy shapes

squeeze tight my eyes the stars reveal,

*

between unfolds,   we take our measure,
; vagaries of snow: flakes, hoarfrost,

graupel, polycrystals
                         ; submissible, an aesthetic experience,

at windows; door blocker, stitched
           from old socks, litter; held

                         to block the draft,

*

     Aoife's bare hand   , cold

*

imagine language   , not in service
, but in practice: a living, breathing

     , akin to snow; the

accident, terrible,   cornice, crust, the
megadunes,

           she drops her mitts, and yet again,
the tumulus,

the embodiment of climates,   conscience
    , hard-hearted; pure

as the driven,

              so to speak; rabbits
paw-print lineage; observing laws

      of gravity, natural selection;

of burrows; trace,
              the fragmentation
    adds a charge

this pool, contracts   , a tiny surface
, pine needles   held
                   in ice,

twelfth night; three hundred sheltered days
or more,

              as the breeze, then; ripples frost

*

facing page,   and truth,

*

what chords,   reveal; she plucks
       the ukulele; strings,

a shaping metaphor for commonplace,

the slopes of the Ottawa Valley; ripple marks, a snow
    barchan,
                sun cups

            willful difficulty, cultivated
for effect,
                , an arm across
    the doorframe, shoulder

*

the sky is blue; the sky
is blue,

*

the mark of which, is that
the world is turning,

a poem, in which   a stay, against time
, the falling snow

                    , a certain height
of archived elements

; protecting, clearing capital;   , a snow plow
range, a rage

the children, laptop   ; school ends,
        YouTube, they devolve;

from action, action,   , replicate,

*

a diagonal   ; impossible to write,

Rose writes a book   about a girl
        and a witch,   ; Aoife

on ukulele, a song
about a gnome who falls in love, and

        it becomes a whole thing, cross

-legged on my office floor,

*

abandoned toques appear   in main floor
bathroom,
  ; none will admit to,

unfurls; what   days have pulled from sleep; the universe
        , this weighted blanket,

Christine attempts as murder weapon,

                        , the grey pallor of
                        this low-weather system,

hard enough   , to lift my eyes,

to lift my eyes to rest,

*

we shall live in the house   , and snow
and I will write my book,

and you are in this book,
and the children are in this book,

and the snow is in this book,
and the house is in this book,

and I will sit with my book,

tsunami ;   and the doomed palace,
        Lego-sharp,   a foil

inside the courtyard   of a bull; a season
    of witchcraft, green-skinned aliens, the

            stitch of their self-directed crafts,

*

what one makes of Pessoa;   the shape of him,

inchoate's   iambic road,

        and: knowing less, and less

*

in relation, and pursuit,

make sure all words are spelled

                        , correct

the nakedness of snow   , and words
, a rain of punctuation

                    disregarding sense; the materiality

of precipitation; footprints, new and untouched, paws

          the base of withered apple tree; mail carrier

lines from one side, door, diagonal; a pulsating rush
of orange plows,
                              a gathering
of letters,
                        ; disruption
      of global climate,

*

to speak, then, of the weather

Acknowledgments

Some of these poems appeared in print and/or online on the author's blog and in *The Peter F Yacht Club* (Ottawa ON), as well as the chapbooks *snow day* (above/ground press, 2018) and *Somewhere in-between / cloud* (above/ground press, 2019). The poem "What they write in the snow" was included in the first issue of Julian Day's *+doc: a journal of longer poems* (Winnipeg MB: null pointer press, summer 2021). "for my fifty-first year," appeared as *the great silence of the poetic line* through Derek Beaulieu's № Press (Banff AB) in an edition of fifty copies, July 26, 2024. "snow day" also appeared in full in the anthology *GROUNDWORK: the best of the third decade of above/ground press 2013-2023* (Halifax NS/Fredericton NB/Picton ON: Invisible Publishing, 2023). My thanks to all the editors, publishers and social media involved.

"Snow day": The Kate Greenstreet quote comes from *The End of Something* (Ahsahta Press, 2017). The Anna Gurton-Wachter quote comes from *MOTHER OF ALL* (above/ground press, 2018), later included in her *Utopia Pipe Dream Memory* (Ugly Duckling Presse, 2019). This sequence is dedicated to Anna Gurton-Wachter. Composed January 11-March 14, 2019.

"Somewhere in-between / cloud" was composed for and published as part of Dusie Kollektiv 9: "Somewhere in the Cloud and Inbetween"—A Tribute to Marthe Reed (1958-2018) as an unofficial/official element of the New Orleans Poetry Festival, April 18-21, 2019. Much thanks to Susana Gardner for her ongoing support. This poem,

in places, utilizes the occasional word and phrase from the late
Marthe Reed (as well as a fragment quoted from Timothy Morton),
including from her co-editor afterward, "'Somewhere Inbetween'
: Speaking-Through Contiguity" from *Counter-Desecration: A
Glossary for Writing Within the Anthropocene*, edited by Linda
Russo and Marthe Reed (Middletown CT: Wesleyan University
Press, 2018). Brilliant thanks to Christine McNair, whose edits
helped find final shape.

"What they write in the snow" was composed from January 4
to 15, 2021, and is dedicated to Rose and Aoife; for Christine.

This book is for Michael Dennis (1956-2020): mentor, friend
and peer.

no liquor on board / and lots of catching up to do
Michael Dennis, *Fade to Blue* (Vancouver BC: Pulp Press, 1988)

January 11, 2018—January 30, 2021
2423 Alta Vista Drive, Ottawa

Born in Ottawa, Canada's glorious capital city, ROB MCLENNAN currently lives in Ottawa, where he is home full-time with the two wee girls he shares with Christine McNair. The author of more than thirty trade books of poetry, fiction and non-fiction, he won the John Newlove Poetry Award in 2010, the Council for the Arts in Ottawa Mid-Career Award in 2014, and was longlisted for the CBC Poetry Prize in 2012 and 2017. In March, 2016, he was inducted into the VERSe Ottawa Hall of Honour. His most recent titles include *a river runs through it: a writing diary* (Spuyten Duyvil, 2025), *On Beauty: stories* (University of Alberta Press, 2024) and the anthology *groundworks: the best of the third decade of above/ground press 2013-2023* (Invisible Publishing, 2023). Later this year sees the publication of *the book of sentences* (University of Calgary Press), his follow-up to *the book of smaller* (University of Calgary Press, 2022). An editor and publisher, he runs above/ground press, *periodicities: a journal of poetry and poetics* (periodicityjournal.blogspot.com) and *Touch the Donkey* (touchthedonkey. blogspot.com). He is editor of *my (small press) writing day,* and an editor/managing editor of *many gendered mothers.* The current Artistic Director of VERSeFest: Ottawa's International Poetry Festival, he spent the 2007-8 academic year in Edmonton as writer-in-residence at the University of Alberta, and regularly posts reviews, essays, interviews and other notices at robmclennan.blogspot.com.

www.ingramcontent.com/pod-product-compliance
Lightning Source LLC
Chambersburg PA
CBHW030507130626
46549CB00007B/2880